THE PLÜG

PURPOSEFUL LIVING UNTO GOD

A 60 Day Devotional For Young Adults

By: Shardae Pressley

THE PLUG - 60 DAY DEVOTIONAL

B4BG Publishing
info@B4BGPublishing.com

Printed in the United States of America
Cover Design: Hakaba Designs

Publisher's Cataloging-in-Publication data
Pressley, Shardae
The Plug : 60 Day Devotional for Young Adults / Shardae Pressley
ISBN 978-0-9995609-0-7

To my parents Kirk & Vanessa Pressley:

I dedicate this book to you. Thank you for daily devotion and a lifetime of dedication. You've taught me that with God nothing is impossible and that living for Christ can provide a lifetime that is nothing less than lit.

PURPOSEFUL LIVING UNTO GOD

TO: _Krislyn McClair_

FROM: _[signature]_

DATE: _____

NOTE: _Kris! Thank you so much for your continued love & support! It means so much to me!_

HOW TO USE

Darkness.

There's something comforting about the absence of light when you are content to sleep. There is no inclination of being wasteful when time seems not to exist. The dark makes it effortless to disregard blatant objects in your immediate area even when they are a detriment to your success. So what pull's us out of the darkness? A curiosity for the thing we can not see but can't help but hear.

Connection.

There's a jolting shock that happens whenever light meets darkness. It's a jarring feeling to go from one state to another with such force. It's in that moment that a true decision must be made. You either allow the senses to take time to adjust or to reject the temporary discomfort and return to the darkness.

Light.

But if you should just so happen to get through the process of connecting, what comes next is an influx of light. A clarity that can only be experienced and is too overwhelming to be put into words. Illumination on the level of revelation that changes your life.

This isn't your grandma's devotional book. It wasn't written for leisurely reading, or to add to a collection. It was written for transformation. It was written to take you out of the darkness and connect you to the light.

TABLE OF CONTENTS

10 Days of
IDENTITY

Picked on Purpose.

DAY 1: IDENTITY CHARGE UP

Ephesians 1:4-5 (NIV)
4 For he chose us in him before the creation of the world to be holy and blameless in his sight. In love 5 he predestined us for adoption to sonship through Jesus Christ, in accordance with his pleasure and will.

You are not a happenstance. **YOU, are not an accident**. You were "chose". Some people don't plan to have children. It just happens and they adjust life accordingly. Not God. He adopted you. You were planned for. That means that what God did was on purpose. He accepted you into his family on purpose. Being adopted into "sonship" is important because in jewish custom, you can not denounce adopted children…because you chose them. Adoption takes legal documentation and agreement to provide care. That's what God did…on purpose.

You're trying to keep a PROMISE you made to God,
All he wants is you to BELIEVE the one he made you.

DAY 2: IDENTITY CHARGE UP

Philippians 3:9 (NIV)
9 and be found in him, not having a righteousness of my own that comes from the law, but that which is through faith in Christ–the righteousness that comes from God on the basis of faith.

YOU are in right standing with God. Right standing means that God is not in a bad mood as far as you're concerned. What put you in right standing? Jesus! You know what that means? If your actions didn't put you in right standing, they can't take you out of right standing. That "right standing" is because of what God has done. Your faith in what he has done is enough to access all the promises and blessings on your life. Don't get caught up in the fact that sometimes you miss the mark. Shame is a distraction from the truth. The truth is the marks Jesus still has from the crucification paid for every mark you would miss.

Stop _tripping_ over sins God stepped on and threw away.

DAY 3: IDENTITY CHARGE UP

Micah 7:18-19 (NLT)
18 Where is another God like you, who pardons the guilt of the remnant, overlooking the sins of his special people? You will not stay angry with your people forever, because you delight in showing unfailing love.
19 Once again you will have compassion on us. You will trample our sins under your feet and throw them into the depths of the ocean!

Sin isn't what keeps God from you. As a matter of fact, it was sin that caused him to give his very best gift...Forgiveness. Through that gift, **YOU are forgiven**. God doesn't dwell on your sin. Instead, he sees you as faultless, blameless and spotless. God doesn't dwell on your mistakes and you shouldn't dwell on them either. Focus on the way God sees you and allow him to transform you into the image he sees.

God's Love Outweighs your ability

to be lovable.

DAY 4: IDENTITY CHARGE UP

Romans 8:39 (GNT)
39 neither the world above nor the world below—there is nothing in all creation that will ever be able to separate us from the love of God which is ours through Christ Jesus our Lord.

We are taught that love should be a reciprocal situation. We are taught not to cross oceans for people who wouldn't jump over puddles. That is not what God teaches us. In God, **You are loved**; before you choose him. The word says that, "God so loved the world that he gave his only begotten son." He didn't love those who were saved, he loved <u>everyone</u> so that we all would have the opportunity to be saved. His love for us far outweighs our ability to ever deserve that kind of love. He extended his love before we knew we needed it, that's how much he loves us.

THE RULES DIDN'T WORK...

THAT'S WHY GOD GAVE YOU THIS RELATIONSHIP

DAY 5: IDENTITY CHARGE UP

Romans 8:3 (NLT)
3 The law of Moses was unable to save us because of the weakness of our sinful nature. So God did what the law could not do. He sent his own Son in a body like the bodies we sinners have. And in that body God declared an end to sin's control over us by giving his Son as a sacrifice for our sins.

Stop memorizing rules. **You are in a relationship** with a God who never intends on breaking up with you. The commandments that were given in the day of Moses didn't allow for one on one direction from the God who gave them. This new agreement that he has through Jesus allows for him to be one on one with every person that will receive him. You can not do this alone and God is right there to help.

People are **confused** by Christianity
because the Christians
don't look like Christ.

DAY 6: IDENTITY CHARGE UP

Matthew 11:19 (NLT)
"Jesus, on the other hand, feasts and drinks, and you say, 'He's a glutton and a drunkard, and a friend of tax collectors and other sinners!' But wisdom is shown to be right by its results."

I wish church focused more on Christ's life before the cross. The cross is arguably the most important part of his life, however to pick 3 days out of his 33 years of life to solely focus on is a bit unfair. I like the part of Christ's life where he was kid who ran off for a few days and his parents were looking all over for him. I like the part of his life where he shared his secrets and his fears with his squad (or disciples). I like the part where a prostitute was washing his feet and everyone in the room met her with judgement while he met her with love. We focus on how supernatural Jesus was, but let us not neglect that he was also human the whole time. It is that truth that indeed gives us hope for how to live life in this world. **You are just like Jesus**, and studying his life gives you a first hand account on the authority you have and how to overcome all the obstacles that you will face.

THE REAL TRICK OF THE ENEMY IS ALLOWING HIM TO MAKE YOU PAY FOR SOMETHING GOD ALREADY GAVE YOU.

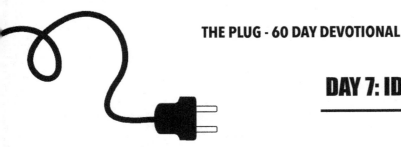

DAY 7: IDENTITY CHARGE UP

Ephesians 2:8-9 (GNT)
8-9 For it is by God's grace that you have been saved through faith. It is not the result of your own efforts, but God's gift, so that no one can boast about it.

You could never afford what it costs to be saved; which is why God sent Jesus Christ to pay for it on your behalf. Picture this: Your mother places a carry-out order for you at your favorite Chinese place and she pays for it on her debit card. You believe your mother placed the order (that's what faith is…belief) so you go to the Chinese place to pick up the order. When you get there, the cashier asks you for money. That's what Satan does. He tries to make you doubt that God already paid for your salvation. That's a lie! **Your salvation is paid for** once you believe in what God has done through Christ. There is no more trying to act "good enough" or "being perfect enough" to qualify for what was given as a gift. Your responsibility is only to receive what has already been done. Don't allow the enemy to fool you into believing you're on the hook for saving yourself. God handled that.

SOMETIMES I TRY TO SQUEEZE BACK INTO WHO I USED TO BE.

I NEVER FIT THO.

DAY 8: IDENTITY CHARGE UP

2 Corinthians 5:17 (NLT)
17 This means that anyone who belongs to Christ has become a new person. The old life is gone; a new life has begun!

Do you feel like you're changing? You should. **You are a new creation** once you accept Christ. That "new" feeling of becoming someone else is stemming from the Holy Spirit. That spirit, which is literally the spirit of God, is now inside of you. I always looked at salvation as having a permanent roommate. Your opinion is no longer alone now. You have company. That "company" now influences the decisions you make and the paths you take. That "company" will work in conjunction with you renewing your mind through the word of God to turn you into God's original intent. That "company" will pursue you and challenge you until you can no longer settle for what you were before God set up residence in your life.

People look at you strange and say you changed; like you can encounter God and stay the same.

DAY 9: IDENTITY CHARGE UP

Romans 12:2 (NLT)
2 ...but let God transform you into a new person by changing the way you think. Then you will learn to know God's will for you, which is good and pleasing and perfect.

Whether it's developing pictures or developing a butterfly from a caterpillar, transformation requires a specific process. Our transformation in Christ can be uncomfortable as God begins to challenge what we knew to be true. Our process is rooted in changing the way that we think. It requires us to give up the perceptions we have and to see the world from the lens of the word. The reason that can be difficult is because we are confronted with continuing to see things as we have always seen them, or to believe in the promises of God that he begins to show us in his word. I've found that the longer you expose and submerge yourself in the scriptures, the word always wins! It's like the caterpillar; so long as it stays in the cocoon, it is bound to become a butterfly. **You are transforming.** Don't stop renewing your mind until you see what God has said.

29

I'M NOT SAYING THERE WON'T BE A BATTLE

WHAT I'M SAYING IS YOU CAN'T BE BEAT

DAY 10: IDENTITY CHARGE UP

2 Chronicles 20:17 (NLT)
17 But you will not even need to fight. Take your positions; then stand still and watch the Lord's victory. He is with you, O people of Judah and Jerusalem. Do not be afraid or discouraged. Go out against them tomorrow, for the Lord is with you!"

You are in a fixed fight. Every battle you will face, God has already won. I know it may look like you are losing and everything around you points to complete defeat, but God will not let you down. It reminds me of being bullied as a child and how I would run home and tell my older brother. In the moment of conflict, right as I began to panic I would remember that there was someone who was bigger than me and strong enough to fight my battles for me. That's what God does for you. When you are facing an opponent, be it spiritual or natural, realize that there is someone in your corner who is bigger, who is stronger. Run home and tell God all about it and allow him to step in and manifest the victory.

IDENTITY: FULLY CHARGED CONFESSIONS

1. I AM NOT AN ACCIDENT

2. I AM IN RIGHT STANDING WITH GOD

3. I AM FORGIVEN

4. I AM LOVED

5. I AM IN A RELATIONSHIP WITH GOD

6. I AM JUST LIKE JESUS

7. MY SALVATION IS PAID FOR

8. I AM A NEW CREATION

9. I AM TRANSFORMING

10. I AM VICTORIOUS

CREATE YOUR OWN IDENTITY CONFESSIONS:

_____

_____

_____

_____

_____

_____

_____

_____

10 Days of
PURPOSE

Don't waste time positioning yourself to be picked. God will send for you. Stay in the field.

DAY 1: PURPOSE CHARGE UP

1 Samuel 16:11-12 (NLT)
11 Then Samuel asked, "Are these all the sons you have?"
"There is still the youngest," Jesse replied. "But he's out in the fields
watching the sheep and goats." "Send for him at once," Samuel said. "We
will not sit down to eat until he arrives." 12 So Jesse sent for him. He was
dark and handsome, with beautiful eyes. And the Lord said, "This is the
one; anoint him."

When you become passionate about your purpose, it will cause you to proceed without a platform. God looks for those types of people who are operating in their purpose and he puts them in position. God is able to find you even when you're not featured. Your purpose will cause God to promote you when it's time. God will look over the line up just to come and get you; the same way he did with David. You don't have to position yourself to be seen, stay in the field.

WHAT GOD PUT IN YOU
IS EQUIPPED TO HANDLE
ANYTHING
THAT COMES AT YOU

DAY 2: PURPOSE CHARGE UP

Hebrews 13:20-21 (NLT)
20 Now may the God of peace..21 may he equip you with all you need for doing his will. May he produce in you, through the power of Jesus Christ, every good thing that is pleasing to him. All glory to him forever and ever! Amen.

I know it feels big and everything around you is saying you don't have what it takes. Guess what? It is huge and you don't have what it takes in your own strength...but with God nothing can stop you. Your purpose has a God guarantee.   God has equipped you and will continue to equip you with everything you need to fulfill the purpose that he has given to you. He will provide the wisdom and the strategy to overcome every obstacle that looks like it's standing in the way.

I'm done writing my own plan. I'm ready to read the one God already wrote.

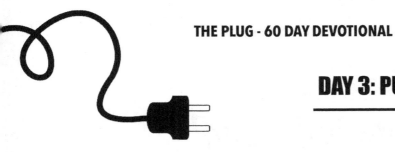

DAY 3: PURPOSE CHARGE UP

Luke 9:23 (ERV)
23 Jesus continued to say to all of them, "Any of you who want to be my follower must stop thinking about yourself and what you want. You must be willing to carry the cross that is given to you every day for following me.

Sometimes purpose can end up buried beneath what's popular. This world feeds you it's ideas and ideologies in heavy doses. Our initial purpose can become convoluted by opportunities that arise as we are on our way. It's easy to end up on a path that was paved by good intentions and strong pushes from those around you. Your purpose requires making a choice. You have to choose to walk in the plans that God has called you to and walk away from "good" things that may not be "God" things.

You will want
to do what
everyone else is doing...

DAY 4: PURPOSE CHARGE UP

Romans 12:4 (ERV)
4 Each one of us has one body, and that body has many parts. These parts don't all do the same thing.

There's this saying that "birds of a feather flock together," which tends to be true. What the saying doesn't specify is that even if the birds are of the same feather, they may not fly the same. It's important to understand that although you may have the same mission as someone else, your purpose has a specific method. One of my favorites from the Bible is David. David was destined to be a great warrior and king. In his first battle, he tried to fight like everyone else. He put on armor and they gave him a sword to go out and fight Goliath. He paused for a moment, took everything off and decided to use his sling shot and stones instead. Why would he do that? Because that was the method for his mission. No matter how everyone else was fighting, he understood it would not work for him unless he did it the way he knew to do it. There is grace that is available for the way in which you are supposed to pursue your purpose. Stop looking around at everyone else and look to God to show you.

You can't talk God out of what he already decided to do with you

DAY 5: PURPOSE CHARGE UP

Exodus 4:13-15 (ERV)
13 But Moses said, "My Lord, I beg you to send someone else, not me."
14 Then the Lord became angry with Moses and said, "All right! I'll give
you someone to help you...15 So I will tell you what to tell him, and I
will help both of you to speak well, and I will tell you what to do.

One of the dopest things about God is that he doesn't create anything without first establishing the purpose of it. In Jeremiah, scripture tells us that before we were formed in our mother's wombs he knew us and he predestined us. Your purpose is predestined. Just like Jesus, your purpose was decided before God put you here in the earth. You know what that means? It means you don't need permission to pursue it. You never have to beg for anyone on earth to agree with what God has already assigned. God's not making up his mind about you; he settled it before he sent you and no one (not even you) can talk him out of it.

Gotta stop committing to things God never called you to.

DAY 6: PURPOSE CHARGE UP

PSALM 127:1 (KJV)
"Unless the LORD builds the house, They labor in vain who build it..."

Satan does not appear in the way we would think. He doesn't come in the form of fire and brimstone or as a monster that's under the bed. No. Satan comes as a distraction. He slips in as a suggestion. He provides you with "ideas"...good ideas. Satan doesn't mind you working, so long as you aren't working on what God gave you to do. The enemy wants you to labor in vain. It is his desire that you starve the vision that God gave you and feed aimless pursuits he causes you to believe are so important. Your purpose requires you to protect your vision. The word instructs us to write our vision and to make it plain so that we are assured in what we are supposed to be carrying out. Without protecting our vision and revisiting the instructions God gave, we can often find ourselves working on the "good" idea that's not a "God' idea. No more wasting time, you have a purpose to tend to.

I KNOW IT HURTS NOW, BUT IT WILL HELP YOU LATER

DAY 7: PURPOSE CHARGE UP

Genesis 50:20 (ESV)
20 As for you, you meant evil against me, but God meant it for good, to bring it about that many people should be kept alive, as they are today.

Christianity doesn't stop us from experiencing the hurt and pain that comes from life. I wish I could tell you that walking with God will provide you a lifetime of living unscathed. It wont. Pain is often the incubator that gives birth to purpose. Pain is the tangible evidence that you are equipped for the project God has assigned you to. It gives you credibility in a circle that is in need of your calling. I'll never forget going through one of the most painful experiences in my life and asking God, "why me?" I remember hearing a still small voice saying, "Because people are gong to come to you with questions, and you are going to have to have the answers." The pain that you go through will allow you to have the answers when you are walking in your purpose. God is not the author of pain, but he is the master of using it when writing your story. Your pain is what gives your purpose power. It is what connects you to those you will one day help.

Copying their tactics wont work. Use the tools God gave you.

DAY 8: PURPOSE CHARGE UP

1 Samuel 17:39 (NLT)
"David strapped Saul's sword over the armor and tried to walk, but he couldn't, because he wasn't used to wearing them. "I can't fight with all this," he said to Saul. "I'm not used to it." So he took it all off."

I'm the biggest coffee drinker I know. Therefore before settling on how I get my daily dose, I tried all my options. I tried the machine that takes the pods. I tried using the filter and the coffee pot. I tried using the espresso machine. I settled for using the Starbucks drive thru. You know what they all have in common? They all have the ability to provide me with coffee. They all, at their core, have the same exact purpose but are equipped to execute that purpose differently. That's how living a purpose filled life can tend to be. Many people will have the same purpose as you but equipped by God to execute that purpose a certain way for a certain group of people. What do you think would happen if I put a coffee pod inside a coffee pot? Absolutely nothing. Don't look around for instruction on how to execute your purpose, look up. Your purpose comes with specific preparation. Don't copy someone else when the execution that God has gifted you with is custom.

51

God Keeps Calling Until You Answer

DAY 9: PURPOSE CHARGE UP

1 Samuel 3:10 (KJV)
10 And the Lord came, and stood, and called as at other times, Samuel! Samuel! Then Samuel answered, Speak; for thy servant heareth.

I'm not saying that God is a nag, but I am saying that he is so invested in you fulfilling the call on your life that he will stop at nothing to get your attention. Your purpose is important to God! He is a manufacturer and he is highly invested in insuring that what he created, does exactly what he created it for. I know sometimes it feels like it doesn't matter one way or the other if you succeed, but the truth is God made an agreement with you that so long as you're seeking him, he refuses to let you fail. No matter how many times he has to repair the parts inside, he will go to extreme lengths to make certain the person you become is fulfilling the purpose he planned for when he placed you in the earth. His name and his word is on the line and he has made it known that his words will not return to him void. That overbearing feeling you're experiencing to do that "thing" is God calling you. It's time to answer.

Stop Giving your time to people sent to distract you from your God given task.

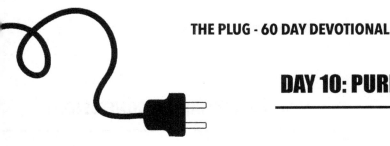

DAY 10: PURPOSE CHARGE UP

Nehemiah 6:3 (KJV)
3 And I sent messengers unto them, saying, I am doing a great work, so that I cannot come down: why should the work cease, whilst I leave it, and come down to you?

You will get there if you keep going. The thing about purpose is that it's God's job to bring it pass and your job to submit to the process. When processes are cut short, the product is never finished. What's stopping you from finishing? Sometimes it's giving your attention to a person or to an activity that is hindering your productivity. In this season of pursuing your purpose, it's ok to say "No". It's ok to turn down opportunities and invitations that are in direct opposition to you finishing. Imagine if a caterpillar were in a cocoon and came out every time someone approached. It would never become a butterfly. Your purpose requires you to tell people "no" so that you can make room to give God a "yes" to what he is calling you to.

PURPOSE: FULLY CHARGED CONFESSIONS

1. MY PURPOSE WILL CAUSE GOD TO PROMOTE ME WHEN IT'S TIME

2. MY PURPOSE HAS A GOD GUARANTEE

3. I MAKE THE CORRECT CHOICES CONCERNING MY PURPOSE

4. GOD GIVES ME WISDOM ABOUT THE SPECIFIC METHOD FOR MY PURPOSE

5. MY PURPOSE IS PREDESTINED

6. I PROTECT MY VISION FOR MY PURPOSE

7. MY PAIN GIVES MY PURPOSE POWER

8. I AM PREPARED FOR MY PURPOSE

9. MY PURPOSE IS IMPORTANT TO GOD

10. I AM NOT AFRAID TO TELL PEOPLE "NO" SO THAT I CAN COMPLETE MY PURPOSE

CREATE YOUR OWN PURPOSE CONFESSIONS:

_____

_____

_____

_____

_____

_____

_____

_____

10 Days of
TRANSITION

God will order your steps but you've got to move your feet

DAY 1: TRANSITION CHARGE UP

Genesis 12:1 (GNT)
12 The Lord said to Abram, "Leave your country, your relatives, and your father's home, and go to a land that I am going to show you.

Once you know who you are, and you know what you are called to do, there comes a point when you will be required to move into position so that you can see God's plan. So many times in the word God says to the people he's chosen to go to a certain place and he will show them or tell them what to do. In your life that may be moving into a new job or moving into a new relationship or even moving to a new city. Whatever it is, God calls us to take the first step without being able to see the entire staircase. Sometimes God doesn't give you a paragraph, he just gives you a word. Transition requires you to move on the word you have. I think God knows that if we knew the extent of what we would encounter, we would forgo starting altogether. 1 step at a time...get moving.

Sometimes seeing is a matter of

DAY 2: TRANSITION CHARGE UP

Psalms 119:105 (KJV)
"Your word is a lamp to guide my feet and a light for my path."

I've been going to the eye doctor since I was 2. The process for me has become a bit redundant. I'm totally over the plain white walls and my legs sticking to the doctor's chair while they run through every frame. "Better One...or Two?" The interesting thing about that test is that the figures on the wall never change. However, the glass in front of your eyes dictates what you are able to see. That's how God's word can be. Before you move forward with clarity in your assignment, ask yourself what filter is between you and the word of God? Transitioning into the next season is dictated by your perception of God's word. Is the word something to JUST make you feel better? That's a bad filter. Is the word something to make you look good because you can recite it? That's not a good filter. The bible tells us the word is bread and seed. The word is the means by which we live and produce a harvest in our lives. Until you shift your mind in seeing it that way, your assignment will always be a bit blurry.

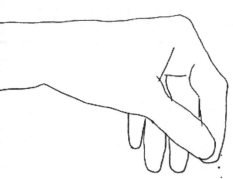

I'm Just Gonna Let God Do His Thing

DAY 3: TRANSITION CHARGE UP

Philippians 2:13 (NIV)
"For it is God who works in you to will and to act in order to fulfill his good purpose"

God is going to work through you so that you get there. Transition requires a willingness to relinquish control so that God can work through you. God is the GPS and solely responsible for the directions to get you from "point A" to "point B". All you are required to do is pay attention and trust (believe in/rely on) the directions. You are required to look at that GPS so intently that you will not miss a turn. You are required to allow that GPS to do all the work and simply follow the turn by turn navigation.

But just incase you happen to go down the wrong street, allow it to recalibrate and get you on the right path. He's working it out so you can walk it out.

Same Doors.
New Keys.

DAY 4: TRANSITION CHARGE UP

Exodus 4:19 (GNT)
¹⁹ While Moses was still in Midian, the Lord said to him, "Go back to Egypt, for all those who wanted to kill you are dead."

Want to know how to tell if you've truly transitioned? Passing the test comes when you can give a familiar scenario an unfamiliar response.

Can you be put in the same scenario that you thought you'd left behind and meet it with a new mindset? Transition may require you to re-encounter the same thing with a new attitude. God saves you so that he can send you. Those people, places and things that you thought you left behind, God will send you back for them; because believe it or not, he loves them too. You're going to walk into the same places, but you will be different. When you go back, you will be confident that the enemy you once faced, does not have the power to destroy you any longer.

**Everything will be falling apart,
but everything is coming together.**

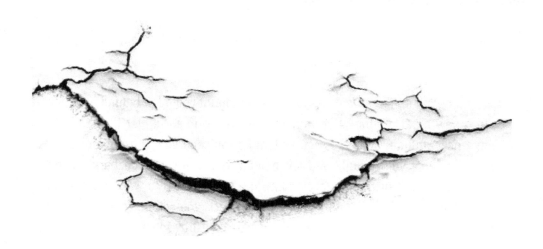

DAY 5: TRANSITION CHARGE UP

Romans 8:28 (GNT)
28 We know that in all things God works for good with those who love him, those whom he has called according to his purpose.

Transition can be difficult because you are no longer what you once were and you are not yet what you are becoming. It's an uncomfortable feeling and an uncomfortable process.

There's a story in the bible where the children of Israel were transitioning. They'd been freed from Egypt but they weren't delivered into the Promised Land just yet. That's what transitioning into purpose can feel like. You're detached from some of the people that used to be your closest friends. You don't go to some of the places you loved to go. But here's the thing, God is manifesting all the things he promised. The circle of friends that you need and the new places you will go: are already in motion. Don't be discouraged. Keep Moving.

69

THERE ARE SO MANY MIRACLES IN THE MIDDLE

DAY 6: TRANSITION CHARGE UP

Exodus 16:4 (NIV)
4 The Lord said to Moses, "Now I am going to cause food to rain down from the sky for all of you.

If there is one thing I recall clearly about transition, it is that in this space I have seen the most miracles. Transition is a place of unfamiliarity and can be uncomfortable but that is seemingly the atmosphere where God does his best work. It is where he shows up for you in ways that no one else can. It is the space where he knows exactly what you need and makes it his mission to meet them all.

In this space of "in-between" I challenge you to look for Him providing for you in ways you've never imagined. I believe it is in this space where he will build your trust and dependence on him because you have no other option.

What have you talked yourself out of, that God is trying to bring you into?

DAY 7: TRANSITION CHARGE UP

Numbers 13:32-33 (GNT)
32 So they spread a false report among the Israelites about the land they had explored. They said, "That land doesn't even produce enough to feed the people who live there. Everyone we saw was very tall, 33 and we even saw giants there...

The best part of transitioning is finally moving into the very thing that God promised. However, it doesn't usually feel that way. When moving into a "new" thing we tend to survey the land just like the children of Israel. Instead of walking in with the boldness of belonging and taking hold of exactly what God promised, we seem to find every reason why claiming it is impossible. We look at the challenges and ignore the covering that got us there. We would rather give it up than allow God to walk us through receiving. Whether it's marriage or a new job; the very thing you prayed for may come with giants you never planned for. Giants in the form of issues you never knew about in your spouse; giants in the form of work requirements you have no clue how to conquer. But guess what? God knew about the giants before you arrived, and he's already planned for you to prosper. Don't run away from what God has given you; allow him to give you the wisdom to handle all that it comes with.

73

DAY 8: TRANSITION CHARGE UP

Numbers 14:23 (GNT)
"They will never enter the land which I promised to their ancestors. None of those who have rejected me will ever enter it."

The Merriam – Webster dictionary defines agreement as "an expression (as a settlement, covenant, or contract) of the intent or willingness of two or more parties to bind on specified terms." In business, there is no forward motion of work performed without an "agreement". That's what faith is – agreement. Faith requires you to bind with the terms laid out in God's word so that he can manifest exactly what he said. Moving forward is a matter of you agreeing. In numbers, the word shows us that the children of Israel did not enter because they were not in agreement; they rejected what God had for them. When God calls you to move forward into the next season of promotion, marriage, debt freedom and every other promise, you must agree with the direction he is taking you. I decree that you will agree and move forward.

Trees don't mourn Leaves

DAY 9: TRANSITION CHARGE UP

Mark 5:18-19 (NIV)
¹⁸ As Jesus was getting into the boat, the man who had been demon-possessed begged to go with him. ¹⁹ Jesus did not let him, but said, "Go home to your own people and tell them how much the Lord has done for you, and how he has had mercy on you."

Growing spiritually and walking in love and light will have you feeling like you have to take every single person where God is taking you. Wrong. Not even Jesus allowed everyone to come along for the ride. In a season of transition, God has shown me that sometimes your next season is like this big party that He's throwing and you don't always get a plus 1. Some people that you meet along the way are seasonal. Those people will fall away similar to the way leaves fall from trees. Don't waste your time trying to pick them up. God is the only non-negotiable companion that is required for you to conquer. People can be fickle and their hearts may not consistently advance your cause. God planned for that; he knows how to give you the people you need in the seasons that they are essential. Trust God's pruning process and grow upward, even when people seem to be growing outward.

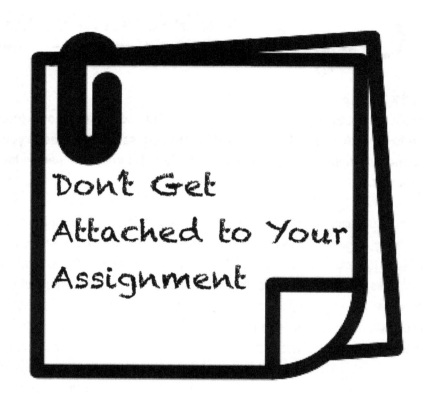

DAY 10: TRANSITION CHARGE UP

1 Samual 16:1 (NIV)
16 The Lord said to Samuel, "How long will you mourn for Saul, since I have rejected him as king over Israel? Fill your horn with oil and be on your way;"

Want to know what keeps you from moving forward? This odd attachment to what used to be your assignment. I love the story of Samuel because he followed God's instructions so gracefully. When God instructed him to anoint Saul, he proceeded. When God said that season was over, Samuel had a hard time. He was not ready to move on just yet. Is that you? Are you stuck on the last word you received? We can find ourselves stuck in Phase 1 because although we've completed our task and learned our lesson, we've somehow attached ourselves to a part of the process. It's literally like staying in kindergarten and not moving on to 1st grade because you are in love with your Kindergarten teacher. When God says you've outgrown your current assignment, do exactly what he told Samuel, "be on your way!"

TRANSITION: FULLY CHARGED CONFESSIONS

1. I ALLOW GOD TO ORDER MY STEPS AS I GO THROUGH TRANSITION

2. I SHIFT MY PERSPECTIVE TO SEE AS GOD SEES

3. I ALLOW GOD TO WORK THROUGH ME TO FULFILL MY PURPOSE

4. I GIVE GOD RESPONSES TO MY EVERYDAY SITUATIONS

5. I BELIEVE ALL THINGS ARE WORKING TOGETHER FOR MY GOOD

6. I EXPECT TO SEE MIRACLES IN THIS SEASON OF MY LIFE

7. I HAVE NO FEAR OF TRANSITIONING INTO EVERYTHING GOD PROMISED

8. I AGREE WITH GOD'S PLAN FOR MY LIFE

9. I ALLOW GOD TO REMOVE ANYTHING THAT SHOULD NOT TRANSITION WITH ME

10. I WILL NOT BE ATTACHED TO MY ASSIGNMENT

CREATE YOUR OWN TRANSITION CONFESSIONS:

_____

_____

_____

_____

_____

_____

_____

_____

10 Days of
ADULTING

"I dont know"

is an excuse

DAY 1: ADULTING CHARGE UP

1 Corinthians 2:16 (NIV)
"Who has known the mind of the Lord so as to instruct him? But we have the mind of Christ."

Maturing in the ways of God is a realization that the only wisdom you don't have, is the wisdom you do not ask for. Once you know your identity and have transitioned into your purpose, there is a responsibility to seek revelation from God. The first step in maturity is acknowledging that you serve a God who seeks to instruct you in all your ways. You are not doing life alone! If you are unclear question God like you know him…because you do. Don't remain in the dark about a situation when you have access to the creator of light.

Don't trip.

LOOK UP

DAY 2: ADULTING CHARGE UP

Psalm 25:15 (MSG)
"If I keep my eyes on GOD, I won't trip over my own feet."

Maturing in Christ means that sometimes, you're tempted to handle new problems the old way. You know, like curse someone out that cut you off in traffic, or telling someone off that's telling your business. I completely understand! Here's the thing though: God's got your back better than you ever could. Go to him about your frustrations with people and circumstances. Cast your cares onto him because there are consequences to our actions. We can often make a bad situation worse, but there are blessings birthed through including him in the scenario. Look to God for the solution, don't get all worked up.

It's tough following a principle, that's why God sent a person.

Focus on the person...

DAY 3: ADULTING CHARGE UP

Galatians 2:16 (NIV)
"Yet we know that a person is made right with God by faith in Jesus Christ, not by obeying the law. And we have believed in Christ...For no one will ever be made right with God by obeying the law."

Living out this "Salvation Lifestyle" can become a bit hectic. It seems as though the deeper you go, the more you question if you're doing the right things, if you're saying the right things, if you're acting the right way. Guess what? Living this life isn't about looking at you at all. The way to thrive in your Christian maturity is realizing in all you do, look at Christ. Look at the forgiveness he's provided for a realization that the world is no longer hinged on your shoulders. Wake up each day not thinking about what you did the day before, but about what God did for you over 2,000 years ago. Commit yourself to renewing your mind in the fact that you were made right through Christ. Understand that no matter how much wrong you've done, it won't change what God already did.

DAY 4: ADULTING CHARGE UP

Colossians 3:1 (NIV)
"Since, then, you have been raised with Christ, set your hearts on things above, where Christ is, seated at the right hand of God."

Maturing in Christ means that you are now seated and heavenly places and aware of the standards that surround your relationship with God. I understand at one point you begged and cried for God to bless you, but now you should be moving toward a position of praying and peaceful patience because of your certainty of His ability to deliver. Walk out your day unashamed of the connection you now have with a God who has prepared and purposed you for this path. Make up your mind to rise above petty and pretentiousness in exchange for favor and anointing.

I'M JUST HERE TO SHOW YOU THEY LIED
WHEN THEY TOLD YOU LIVING FOR GOD
COULDN'T BE LIT.

DAY 5: ADULTING CHARGE UP

Ecclesiastes 8:15 (MSG)
"So I recommend having fun, because there is nothing better for people in this world than to eat, drink, and enjoy life. That way they will experience some happiness along with all the hard work God gives them under the sun."

Christians should be the happiest people on earth. Not because they are better than anyone else but because they have access to everything God promised from the creation of the world. This life is not supposed to be boring. It should be filled with surprises that cause others to ask about the God you serve. The word says, "Signs should follow those who believe." You should expect to see God show up not just at church but also in the drive thru with someone covering your order, or on your job with unexpected promotion, or in your circle with new friends. This life we were given should be greater than we could ask think or imagine! That's what the word tells us and our expectation shouldn't be anything less.

Say your prayers and mind your business.

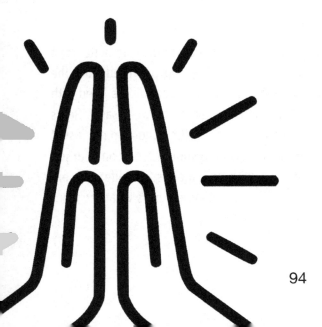

94

DAY 6: ADULTING CHARGE UP

1 Thessalonians 4:11 (MSG)
"Make it your aim to live a peaceable life, to mind your own business, and to earn your own living, just as we told you before."

Maturing in Christ means putting an end to comparison. We all win when we're focused on playing the position we were purposed for. The acceptance of your identity and transitioning into your God given purpose should yield an intense focus on what you are called to do. Comparison is the quickest thief of focus. Who's path are you looking at? Who is causing you to question if you're headed in the right direction? Block them. Mute them. Remove yourself from their presence until their open success doesn't cause you to question your private preparation. Keep your mind on what God is doing in and through you. You're maturing and you don't have time for distractions.

What company are you keeping?

DAY 7: ADULTING CHARGE UP

1 Corinthians 15:33 (NIV)
33 Do not be misled: "Bad company corrupts good character."

Sometimes, renewing your mind and spirit requires renewing your circle. The word tells us that the company you keep is more than important. Company is so important to God that he sent the Holy Spirit to set up permanent residence in your life. The issue arises when the Holy Spirit inside of you, is in constant opposition with everyone around you. Maturing in Christ may mean a change in your circle. It requires you to surround yourself with people who are in agreement so that you can see manifestation. I know it may be hard, but trust that the change they see in you will ignite a change in them. Sometimes our inability to admit we've outgrown a friendship prevents the other person from growing as well. Don't be afraid to separate from people. If the friendship is meant to be, God always knows how to bring it back together at the right time.

Have that
same energy...

DAY 8: ADULTING CHARGE UP

Psalms 37:23 (MSG)
"The LORD directs the steps of the godly. He delights in every detail of their lives."

Have you ever witnessed a person in a one sided relationship? They go the extra mile for their significant other and make public declarations of their love for them, but there's radio silence on the other end. Is that what your relationship with God is like? I'm referring to a relationship where God openly blesses you and you privately praise him. God doesn't want to be confined to the journal on your bedside table. God wants to be actively involved in every area of your life. He wants to be mentioned in conversation and talked to at your office desk when you're trying to figure something out. We love to showcase our affiliations with our alma maters and throw up signs if we are a part of an organization. While maturing in Christ, I challenge you to have the same energy for the God that loved you long before you decided to love him back.

You will never cry a tear that God won't catch

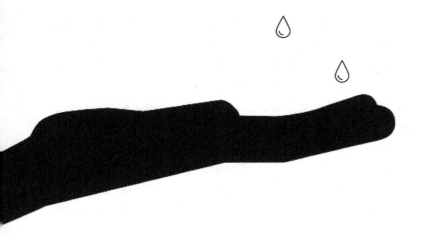

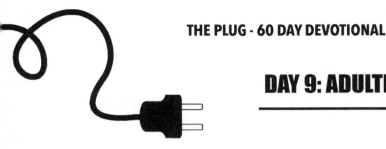

DAY 9: ADULTING CHARGE UP

Psalm 56:8 (NLT)
8 You keep track of all my sorrows. You have collected all my tears in your bottle. You have recorded each one in your book.

If we're being honest, maturing in the things of God will have you in your feelings. I know first hand the frustration of being a new person on the inside and feeling disrespected on the outside. Where you once panicked, you now pray. Where you once fought, you put faith in God to resolve the issue. The relinquishing of control is something that can bring you to tears. God sees you. He sees you maturing and developing and he is keeping track of every single tear that you have cried. He rewards those who diligently seek him and I want you to meditate today on the truth that all of your progress is not in vain.

DO IT FOR THE FRUIT.

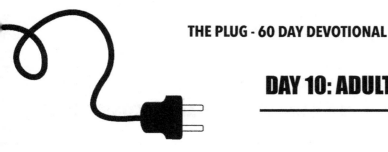

DAY 10: ADULTING CHARGE UP

Matthew 7:16 (KJV)
16 Ye shall know them by their fruits...

The completion of a maturation process yields an ability to produce. Want to know if you are truly matured in God? Look at what you are producing. Is there anything flowing from your life that is evidence that there has been a transformation on the inside of you? Apple trees are planted and from a seed a tree grows but it can benefit no one until the apples appear on the branches. I declare "apples" in your life. I decree that you produce from whatever seed God has planted and in this season it manifests in tangible form to bless someone else. Fruit is always for others. It benefits someone outside of the originating provider. When we mature in Christ, our aim is to benefit someone else with our lives. We should aim to be an introduction to the one who helped us produce the fruit so that someone else will begin producing their own.

ADULTING: FULLY CHARGED CONFESSIONS

1. I HAVE THE MIND OF CHRIST AND HIS WISDOM IN ALL THAT I DO

2. I DO NOT PANIC; I SEEK GOD IN MY DECISION MAKING

3. I MAKE JESUS MY FOCUS AND I LIVE A LIFE PATTERNED AFTER HIS LIFE

4. I SET MY MIND ON THINGS ABOVE

5. I LIVE A LIFE OF FUN AND FAVOR

6. I MIND MY BUSINESS AND DO NOT COMPARE MY PATH

7. I SEEK GOD IN THE COMPANY I KEEP

8. I AM NOT ASHAMED OF MY RELATIONSHIP WITH GOD

9. I LOOK TO GOD FOR COMFORT AND ALLOW HIM TO MEND WHAT IS BROKEN

10. I WILL SEE FRUIT FROM MY LIFE

CREATE YOUR OWN ADULTING CONFESSIONS:

_____

_____

_____

_____

_____

_____

_____

_____

10 Days of
NOT SETTLING

This is the season where you see what you've been saying.

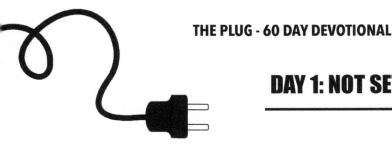

DAY 1: NOT SETTLING CHARGE UP

Job 22:27-28 (KJV)
"Thou shalt make thy prayer unto him, and he shall hear thee. Thou shalt also decree a thing, and it shall be established unto thee."

Sometimes settling is all a matter of what you've been saying. You know who you are, you know what you're called to do, you've been prepared and you've matured in the things of God. Now it's time to see all that He has been saying. The only way to see what God has already said is to ensure you are saying the same things. Is your mouth in agreement with His manifestation? Words are seed and the word of God is a book full of everything you want to grow. Watch your mouth today. Be sure that you want to grow everything that you are placing in the soil of the spirit with the words that are coming out of your mouth. You have the power to frame your world the way God intended it. Focus on the authority of your tongue.

You've gotta believe that you've already got it, more than the voices say you'll never have it...

DAY 2: NOT SETTLING CHARGE UP

2 Peter 1:3 (ESV)
"By his divine power, God has given us EVERYTHING we need pertaining to life and godliness. We have received all of this by coming to know him, the one who called us to himself."

The devil does not take a day off. Every opportunity he has he will create opposition to you receiving everything that God has for you. If he can convince you that God has nothing for you, then 'nothing' is what you will receive. Everything that is coming your way is based on you believing that it is indeed coming. I don't care how many voices in your head say you'll never be completely healed, or say you'll never be prosperous or say you'll never be married, if you can find it in the word then you have a right to those things. Believe in what the word says more than the lies the enemy tells. If need be, go back and read to build yourself up in your belief.

What you want exists. Will you wait for it?

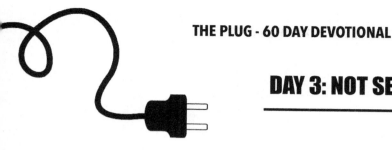

DAY 3: NOT SETTLING CHARGE UP

Isaiah 30:18 (MSG)
"But GOD 's not finished...GOD takes the time to do everything right–
everything. Those who wait around for him are the lucky ones."

My Pastor once said, "patience is faith that lasts a long time." How long can you keep your faith out there? I hope it's until you see exactly what God said. The thing is, God is not bound by time but he knows how to give us what we need at the right time. He works behind the scenes on the hearts of people and mending together situations in ways that our minds could never comprehend. We think that He's keeping us waiting, but really he's working. He's taking the time to ensure what he manifests is perfected. Begin to look at the time spent waiting as time allowed for God to continue adding layers to the blessing that is coming your way.

You know what's worse than sitting still?

Going backwards.

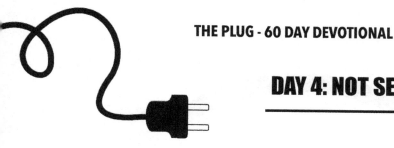

DAY 4: NOT SETTLING CHARGE UP

Jeremiah 7:24 (MSG)
"But my people would not listen to me. They kept doing whatever they wanted, following the stubborn desires of their evil hearts. They went backward instead of forward."

A life with God should go from glory to glory but sometimes when we are not willing to wait to go to the next level, we end up going backward instead. We live in a society where what we want appears instantaneously. To be in a situation where we are required to operate in patience seems irrational. Often times when God is trying to lead us and we feel it's not working out, we take matters into our own hands. That leads us right back to where we came from. When you aren't seeing the progress in your life that you wish to see, be still.

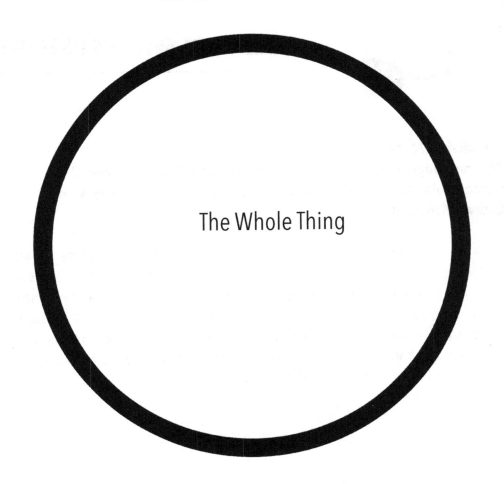

The Whole Thing

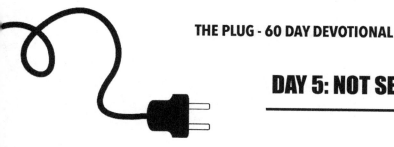

DAY 5: NOT SETTLING CHARGE UP

Romans 8:32 (ESV)
He who did not spare his own Son but gave him up for us all, how will he not also with him graciously give us all things?

We serve a God of "wholeness." Whole means that there is nothing missing and nothing broken. It means that it is ALL there: healing, prosperity, love, and friendships…the list goes on. Many Christians don't demand wholeness. We settle for a piece of what God promised us. Settling for a piece of what God promised is the equivalent of ordering a combo at a drive thru, and driving away without your drink saying, "that's ok, I've got the meal." The drink was paid for too. Your happiness was paid for too. Your debt freedom was paid for too. Your healing was paid for too. Don't accept seeing only a piece of what the word said you could have. Write the scriptures down, and believe to receive everything the blood of Jesus paid for.

Nope.

Bigger.

DAY 6: NOT SETTLING CHARGE UP

Ephesians 3:20 (NKJV)
20 Now to Him who is able to do exceedingly abundantly above all that we ask or think, according to the power that works in us

I don't think I've ever been in a situation where God allowed something to be taken from me and failed to slide through with the upgrade. We serve a God of "exceedingly abundantly" above what we ask or think. We serve a God above our last situation and circumstance. What are you asking? What are you thinking? That's the benchmark that he's going above, but more than that how far are you willing to go to allow him to work through you to achieve what you believe for. Most of the time, the issue isn't how big our imagination is, but we settle when it comes to the availability of God using us to bring the ideas to fruition. I declare that you are available. I believe that you don't settle for big ideas, but that you open yourself to be used to manifest them.

Look at God closing the doors you kept making spare keys to.

DAY 7: NOT SETTLING CHARGE UP

Ephesians 1:11-12 (MSG)
11-12 It's in Christ that we find out who we are and what we are living for. Long before we first heard of Christ and got our hopes up, he had his eye on us, had designs on us for glorious living, part of the overall purpose he is working out in everything and everyone.

It's not hard to tell when you're settling for something that is less than you deserve. But what about when settling has nothing to do with what you deserve and everything to do with what you were created for? The most dangerous type of settling is staying in a "good" place when it's not where you are graced to be. God is the King of closing doors so that you will move into the next room. I don't care how great you were in your last season at your last task, if it's not your final destination, you can't stay there. Today focus on letting go of who you were, and put your full attention on who God is calling you to be.

Don't be Dust...

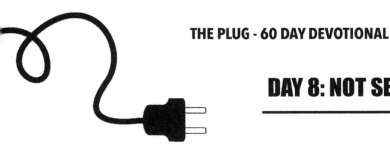

DAY 8: NOT SETTLING CHARGE UP

John 5:8-9 (MSG)
8-9 Jesus said, "Get up, take your bedroll, start walking." The man was healed on the spot. He picked up his bedroll and walked off.

Dust consists of fine particles that come from an array of sources: soil, weather and even human skin. This collection gathers in the atmosphere and begins to lie wherever it falls. Sometimes that's how settling happens. There are times when it is not a result of intentionally following your own selfish desires. Sometimes settling is landing wherever the wind takes you. It is riding the rollercoaster of life without the acknowledgement that you have the authority to control your direction. Being dust is a happenstance of a laissez faire type of lifestyle. Today make up your mind that you will not just allow "life" to happen to you. Get off autopilot and walk out what God has for you.

You're Right, You don't deserve it

DAY 9: NOT SETTLING CHARGE UP

Ephesians 2:8-9 (NIV)
8 For it is by grace you have been saved, through faith–and this is not from yourselves, it is the gift of God– 9 not by works, so that no one can boast.

I've talked myself out of many a blessing because I told myself that I didn't deserve it. I was willing to settle where I was because I couldn't imagine receiving more than what I had after all the mistakes I'd made. Is that you? Do you believe that the promises of God are too good to be true and reject most of the good things that come your way? Well here's the thing: you don't deserve it, that's why it's a gift. Gifts are unearned and every blessing manifested in your life is a testament to how much God loves you, not how much you've done. When you question good relationships, promotion and prosperity, you are mentally placing a cap on what you believe you should be receiving. Settling is forfeiting your gift; passing it on because you feel ashamed to receive it. Today, refuse to settle for what your past says you can have and boldly receive all God has for you.

"And it came to pass..."

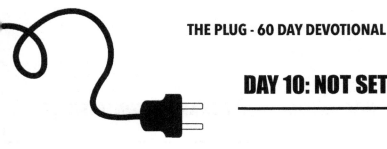

DAY 10: NOT SETTLING CHARGE UP

The phrase, **"and it came to pass," appears 397 times** in the King James Version of the bible. Each time it was written it was utilized in a different context, but the meaning was rooted in the fact that there was an end to a previous circumstance and a new declaration had been established. Today I want you to meditate on the knowledge that not only will God not allow you to settle, but he also will not allow issues to permanently settle in your life. Whatever it is that you are dealing with, it HAS to pass. If the circumstance did not come from God: loneliness, brokenness, poverty, sickness and the list goes on – it cannot stay, it's not allowed to settle! While you are frustrated, in the midst of your tears, understand that the issues you are facing have an expiration date. This season has to complete its course and move on. You are not stuck because those issues do not have the authority to stick to you. There is light at the end of this tunnel; no season is allowed to last forever.

 **NOT SETTLING: FULLY CHARGED CONFESSIONS**

1. I WILL HAVE WHAT I SAY

2. I BELIEVE IN THE PROMISES OF GOD

3. I WILL WAIT TO SEE WHAT GOD HAS PROMISED

4. I AM ANXIOUS FOR NOTHING

5. I BELIEVE TO SEE THE COMPLETE FINISHED WORKS OF GOD IN MY LIFE

6. I FLOW IN THE ABUNDANCE THAT A LIFE IN CHRIST PROVIDES

7. I SEEK THE GOD OPPORTUNITIES

8. I DO NOT SETTLE FOR LESS THAN WHAT IS PROMISED

9. I RELY ON GOD'S GOODNESS AND NOT MY OWN

10. I BELIEVE THAT WHAT GOD SAID WILL COME TO PASS

CREATE YOUR OWN NOT SETTLING CONFESSIONS:

_____

_____

_____

_____

_____

_____

_____

10 Days of
LEGACY BUILDING

The thin line between
ripe and rotten is called
"Time"

DAY 1: LEGACY BUILDING CHARGE UP

Ecclesiastes 3:1 (NIV)
"For everything there is a season, a time for every activity under heaven."

Farmers plant a seed in the ground, thoughtfully water it and tend to it until a harvest comes. Most people get excited about harvest until they realize it requires the act of harvesting. You see, harvesting is the collection process. It is the point where the product has reached its peak and a person must take the time to gather what has been produced. What happens when a person doesn't feel like harvesting? The harvest spoils and must be removed to begin the process again. The seeds inside of you have been tended to and are maturing so that others can benefit. Are you willing to gather all the lessons learned and the preparation to be a benefit to those around you? Or will you let them lie dormant? Make up your mind to use what's inside of you in this season.

Don't Faint.
You have a harvest to get to.

DAY 2: LEGACY BUILDING CHARGE UP

Galatians 6:9 (NIV)
"And let us not be weary in well doing: for in due season we shall reap, if we faint not."

The bible is full of real people telling real stories about their real lives. It is literally like reading someone's journal from over 2000 years ago. Many times when I'm reading, I try to look at it from that perspective. How would I have felt if I were Moses leading a crowd of unappreciative and complaining people? A part of me wants to think that I would have handled it well, but I know in my heart I would have wanted to quit. I am encouraged because what I face is nothing in comparison to what Moses faced. What gives me the right to quit? Just like Moses, there are people attached to the completion of my purpose. Just like Moses there are people relying on you to accomplish what you've been assigned. If Moses didn't get weary and quit why should you? Don't get weary; someone is depending on you to finish.

Not the one you think...

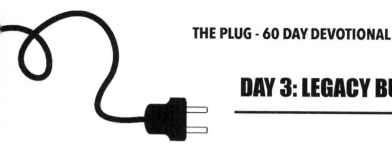

DAY 3: LEGACY BUILDING CHARGE UP

1 Samuel 16:11 (MSG)
¹¹ Then he asked Jesse, "Is this it? Are there no more sons?"
"Well, yes, there's the runt. But he's out tending the sheep."
Samuel ordered Jesse, "Go get him. We're not moving from this spot until he's here."

One thing about God that amazes me is that He puts emphasis on the circumstances and people we overlook. What if your legacy was in the leftovers? Leftovers are meals that were never completely finished and put to the side for later. There are a lot of skills and abilities that we begin with and then put to the side for later. Most of the time, those leftovers go overlooked and end up in the trash. I love the story of David so much because the seed that the father overlooked was the one that carried the legacy. Which one of your seeds are you overlooking? Sometimes the gift or talent we gave up on yields the biggest harvest. Don't throw away the gift you started with at the beginning. Pull it back out and watch God work.

If you don't like the harvest, change the seed.

138

DAY 4: LEGACY BUILDING CHARGE UP

Galatians 6:7 (KJV)

7 Be not deceived; God is not mocked: for whatsoever a man soweth, that shall he also reap.

If you don't like the direction your life is going, you have the power to change it. I believe it is fair to attribute some of your present circumstances to your past trials and tribulations. You did not choose your parents, or your upbringing or your initial atmosphere...but now you can. What will you do with that power? Now that you have matured in the things of Christ, you know that you can, "speak those things that be not, as though they were and it shall come to pass." Where your life goes from this moment is dictated by the decisions you make in this season. Ten percent of life is what happens to you and the other ninety percent is how you handle what has happened. Your present seed directs your future harvest. Choose to sow love. Choose to sow patience. Choose to sow hard word. Others placed the initial seeds that were sown into your life. Now that you are the sower, only put in your ground what you wish to see.

Jesus' blood outweighs your bloodline.

DAY 5: LEGACY BUILDING CHARGE UP

Hebrews 13:12 (KJV)
12 Wherefore Jesus also, that he might sanctify the people with his own blood, suffered without the gate.

Let's talk about the legacy I came from: My mother was a teen mom and my father did not meet his father until later on in his life. My mother was diagnosed with cancer and my father was diagnosed with polycystic kidney disease in his 30s. They defeated the odds and have been married for over 30 years. They both overcame diseases that were supposed to kill them. They both understood that while they came from a bloodline of dysfunction, they were born into a new bloodline. You see, salvation isn't a club it's a family. When the word says that you were adopted into sonship, it means that you are joined with Christ through blood. That blood is stronger than the blood that you were born from. That blood is strong enough to overcome the generational curses and hereditary health issues that the world says should be attached to you.

Are you Hungry Yet?

DAY 6: LEGACY BUILDING CHARGE UP

Proverbs 16:26 (MSG)
Appetite is an incentive to work; hunger makes you work all the harder.

Calling hits you like a hunger pain in the middle of the night. It refuses to let you sleep. It causes discomfort until you take the initiative to feed the "hungry." Sometimes, the hunger comes from a removal of everything you were used to eating. When you experience different avenues of nourishment drying up, often times it's God leading you toward your legacy. The removal of all other options outside of the one you were created for leaves you "hungry." Are you hungry yet? Hunger will cause you to get up and seek out what you need. It wakes you up in the middle of the night and forces you out of comfort. Embrace your hunger today and allow it to be your driving force to your divine destiny.

Consistency is Required to Conquer

DAY 7: LEGACY BUILDING CHARGE UP

2 Corinthians 8:11 (ESV)
[11] So now finish doing it as well, so that your readiness in desiring it may be matched by your completing it out of what you have.

You know what kills your legacy before you've even begun? Instant gratification. I love the ingenuity of the time period we now live. It is refreshing that we have access to information and research in the palms of our hands. We have platforms to release ideas and inventions that receive immediate praise and gratification. The issue with instant gratification is that it delays actual action. You see, research has shown that the amount of endorphins created by that initial praise, is enough for the human psyche. Many people never finish what they started because they received the validation they needed from the "idea" of starting. God shows us in the word that our readiness for what we are purposed to do must be matched by our completion of the purpose. Consistently moving forward is required to conquer in this life. Your legacy depends on your consistency. FINISH!

An example is better than an explanation.

DAY 8: LEGACY BUILDING CHARGE UP

Genesis 45:7 (NIV)
⁷ But God sent me ahead of you to preserve for you a remnant on earth and to save your lives by a great deliverance

I have ended up on my knees asking God for answers more times than I care to admit. There have been situations and circumstances that I thought would never end…but they did. I remember in one of those dark periods asking God "why?" His answer was, "people will have questions, and you have to have answers." In that moment, God taught me that an example is always better than an explanation. Being an example leaves a legacy of answers. Life's experiences cause you to be what the word refers to as a "remnant." To be a remnant means to be the remaining example. That is what legacy is all about: leaving behind an example. God wants your purpose to be produced in the earth in such a way that it becomes an example for others. What you do in the earth becomes an example of God's faithfulness, an example of God's love and an example of God's unfailing power.

We gone be alright!

DAY 9: LEGACY BUILDING CHARGE UP

Proverbs 13:22 (NLV)
22 A good man leaves what he owns for his children's children. The riches of the sinner are stored up for those who are right with God.

Exodus 12:35-36 (GNT)
35 The Israelites had done as Moses had said, and had asked the Egyptians for gold and silver jewelry and for clothes. 36 The Lord made the Egyptians respect the people and give them what they asked for. In this way the Israelites carried away the wealth of the Egyptians.

I used 2 scriptures for today because I want you to understand just how important your financial legacy is to God. I would do you a disservice if I told you that leaving a legacy was only about completing your purpose. It is God's will for you to have nothing missing and nothing broken in every area of your life. The story of the Israelites leaving Egypt shows how God was intentional that his people who were once in bondage not only left slavery but entered into prosperity. Prosperity gives you the ability to make decisions based on the Holy Spirit and not your bills. That is important to God. It is so important that he also tells us in Proverbs that it's his will that the legacy we leave behind is one that also frees generations to come from financial bondage as well.

YOU'RE
A
LEGACY

DAY 10: LEGACY BUILDING CHARGE UP

Isaiah 55:11 (GNT)
11 So also will be the word that I speak– it will not fail to do what I plan for it; it will do everything I send it to do.

I'm so proud of you for making it through this 60-day journey. It is my prayer that you have an understanding of who you are and what you are purposed to do. I decree that you will keep going, mature in the things of God and not accept anything lower than what God has called you to. I declare that you will leave a legacy that impacts the world. The last thing I want to sow into your life is the truth that you are God's legacy. The word tells us that before you were formed in your mother's womb he knew you and spoke over you all that you would become. I want you to root your confidence in the fact that what God spoke will always have the power and anointing to come to pass. His words over your life will not fail so long as you are in agreement with what he has said. I pray that you see it. I beckon to God that he vividly shows you every word he has spoken and believe that you will stand in agreement to see the end that he knew from your beginning.

LEGACY BUILDING: FULLY CHARGED CONFESSIONS

1. I CONSULT GOD ABOUT MY ASSIGNMENT FOR THIS SEASON

2. I WILL NOT FAINT OR BE WEARY IN WELL DOING

3. I DO NOT BELITTLE MY GIFTS AND TALENTS

4. I SHALL HAVE WHAT I SAY

5. I BELIEVE THE BLOOD OF JESUS IS STRONG ENOUGH TO OVERCOME GENERATIONAL CURSES

6. I AM PERSISTENT IN PURSUING MY PURPOSE

7. I AM CONSISTENT AND PRODUCTIVE

8. I WILL LEAVE AN EXAMPLE FOR MY FAMILY

9. ALL IS WELL WITH ME, MY HOUSE AND MY FUTURE

10. I AM A LEGACY

CREATE YOUR OWN LEGACY BUILDING CONFESSIONS:

_____

_____

_____

_____

_____

_____

_____

_____

A note from the Author:
I am proud of you. You made it through the journey!
I'm excited because I know that it is only the beginning.
Xoxo
-Dae

For information and products visit:
ShardaePressley.com

Made in the USA
Columbia, SC
12 July 2018